MAKE AND LEARN

Stories Jesus Told

Elrose Hunter

Illustrated by Jane Taylor

Scripture Union

© 1999 Scripture Union
Text copyright © 1999 Scripture Union
Illustrations copyright © Jane Taylor
First published 1999

Scripture Union, 207–209 Queensway, Bletchley, Milton Keynes MK2 2EB

ISBN 1 85999 275 7

Colour reproduction by Fleet Litho.
Printed in Singapore by Tien Wah Press.

Cover design by Patricia Donnelly Graphic Design.

Contents

Introduction

Jesus was a superb storyteller. In this book we have included many of his stories, retold in language which children can understand.

We are also encouraging them to enter into the story with the creative craft of collage. The pictures in this book were designed with simplicity in mind, using materials which are easily obtainable, if not already to hand in the home. A strong paper or card forms the background for all the designs, and should be robust enough to stand up to all the paint, glue and enthusiasm which the child will apply as the collage proceeds! You can use a heavyweight cartridge paper from any art shop, or sugar paper (which is cheaper), or a panel cut from the nearest cereal packet!

It's probably more important to make sure you have the right paint and glue. Non-toxic paint for children is available in large pots or squeezy bottles from the creative play sections of toy shops and department stores, and many of these are also washable.

You can use a saucer or plate to mix colours up, and have two or three different sized brushes to hand for background and detail work. You don't need a huge amount of artistic skill or finesse for the backgrounds, as most of them are very simple, but it's a good chance to let your child experiment and learn about the variety of effects which can be achieved just by altering the size or shape of a brush.

The glue should also be non-toxic, but needs to be fairly strong for most of the materials, so use the thick white upvc glue which is now also available for children, is non-toxic and easily removed from hands. (Clothes may be another matter, so cover up with old shirts or painting aprons, and supervise the sticking!) This glue is also good for creating special effects (see The Lost Son picture), but if you apply it very thickly you may have to wait an hour or two for it to dry, in which case you might like to do that the night before you plan to paint it, or read the rest of the book while you're waiting...

The rest of the collage materials consist mainly of card, paper, dried grass and twigs, and dried foodstuffs such as rice and pasta. But part of the fun of collage making is in improvisation. Be versatile, and if you haven't got it, try using something else! Children are very imaginative and good with ideas in this area. As long as you make sure your materials aren't actually perishable, then it really doesn't matter what you use as long as you and your child are pleased with the result. This is what being creative is all about. The same thing holds true for artistic ability. If you can't draw donkeys and yours ends up looking like a rabbit, the chances are your child won't notice! And if it doesn't matter to the child, then it really doesn't matter!

A final word about safety. You will know just how much supervision your child needs with paint and glue, as this is largely dependent on age and ability. But do take special care where any use of scissors is required. Children's paper scissors may not be adequate for cutting some of the materials (i.e. stiff card or pasta), so you will need to do those jobs yourself using real grown-up scissors. If you are using a craft knife never leave it within a child's reach, even for a minute. They are very sharp and potentially dangerous, and only adults should use them.

Have fun with the collages!

Jane Taylor

The Lost Sheep

Crowds of people followed Jesus and he taught them about God. They loved to listen to his stories about things that they could see around them. These stories also had a deeper meaning.

One day Jesus told a story about a shepherd and his sheep. This shepherd had a hundred sheep to look after. Every day he would lead them to places where the grass was good. He would watch out for any bears or lions who might attack them. Every night he would lead them back to the safety of the sheepfold.

One evening he found that he had only ninety-nine sheep. One sheep was missing! What had happened to it? Had it wandered away and fallen over a cliff? Had a lion grabbed it?

The shepherd was very worried. He left the ninety-nine sheep and went to look for the lost sheep. He looked among prickly bushes where it might be caught. He called loudly and listened for a bleat from the sheep.

At last he found it on a narrow ledge. He pulled it to safety with his strong shepherd's crook. He lifted the sheep on to his shoulders and carried it back to the flock.

Then he called his friends together. "Come and hear the good news about my lost sheep which I found again!"

Jesus said that people who turn away from God are like that lost sheep. God is like the shepherd who looked for his sheep and was glad when he found it.

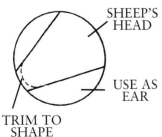

SHEEP'S
HEAD

USE AS
EAR

TRIM TO
SHAPE

How to make the sheep picture
- You will need white card or paper, glue, cotton wool and dried leaves or moss. Paint the background with hills and sky or use coloured papers.
- To make the sheep, cut a rectangle of white card for the body. Curve the top with scissors. Cut up more card for the legs. Stick them in place. Make the head from a circle of card as shown. Glue the head and ear in place.
- Roll small pieces of cotton wool into balls. Glue on to the sheep's body. Add your moss and leaves. Draw a face on your sheep.

The Two Builders

Jesus told a story about two builders.

Once there was a man who wanted to build a house. He chose a place near a river but he dug down deep into the earth until he hit solid rock. It was hard work clearing away all the soft soil but the man was wise. He built his house on the firm rock. Little by little the walls grew. At last the man was able to put on the flat roof and his family moved into the new house.

Then one day heavy rain began to fall from dark clouds. Winds whistled around the house as though they were trying to knock it down. The river rose and overflowed. The water swirled around the house.

"Don't worry," the man told his family. "Our house is strong. It will keep us safe."

There was another man who also wanted to build a house but he was not so wise. He thought, "I'll find a place where the ground is soft. That will make it easy to build my house."

The foolish man built his house and his family moved in. Then the storm came. The rain fell and the winds blew hard. The river overflowed and swirled around the house. It washed away the soft soil and the house shook.

"Quick! Let's get out while we can," called the foolish man.

The family got out just in time. The house crashed down and lay in ruins.

When Jesus told the story, he said, "If you listen to me and do as I say, you'll be just as wise as the man who built on rock."

How to make the house picture
- Draw a house with one door and window. Paint a stormy background.
- Crumple and fold brown paper. Glue down to make the rocks.
- Make the house out of pastry. You will need 140g plain flour, 40 ml cooking oil and 50 ml water. Mix these together to make a dough, adding more water if you need it.
- Roll out thinly and cut into small brick shapes. Place on a floured baking tray and ask an adult to cook it for you in the oven (gas mark 6, 200°C, 400°F) for about ten minutes. When your "bricks" are cool, you can glue them in place carefully. Paint a wooden door and an orange glow in the window to make the house look cosy and warm.

The Lost Coin

One day Jesus told a story about a woman in her home. He did not give her a name but we'll call her Sarah.

Sarah lived in a small house made of mud bricks. There was just one room in the house and it was quite dark because the door was low and there were no windows. Sarah had to light an oil lamp if she wanted to see clearly.

One day Sarah lost one of the ten coins which she wore on a string across her forehead. It was part of the headdress which she had worn since she got married and she was very upset.

Sarah lit the oil lamp and looked on the floor of her house. She couldn't see the coin. She opened the roll of mats which the family slept on in case the coin was inside them. But it wasn't there. She lifted the cooking pots in case it had rolled underneath them but it wasn't there either.

"I suppose I had better sweep the whole house," she said to herself. "It might have rolled into a dark corner."

So she swept carefully into all the corners and suddenly something glinted in the light from the oil lamp.

"There it is!" Sarah said happily and picked up the missing coin. She ran to the door and called to her neighbour. "Hannah! I've found the coin I lost. I'm so pleased I'd like to give a party!"

Jesus said that people are as precious to God as Sarah's coin was to her.

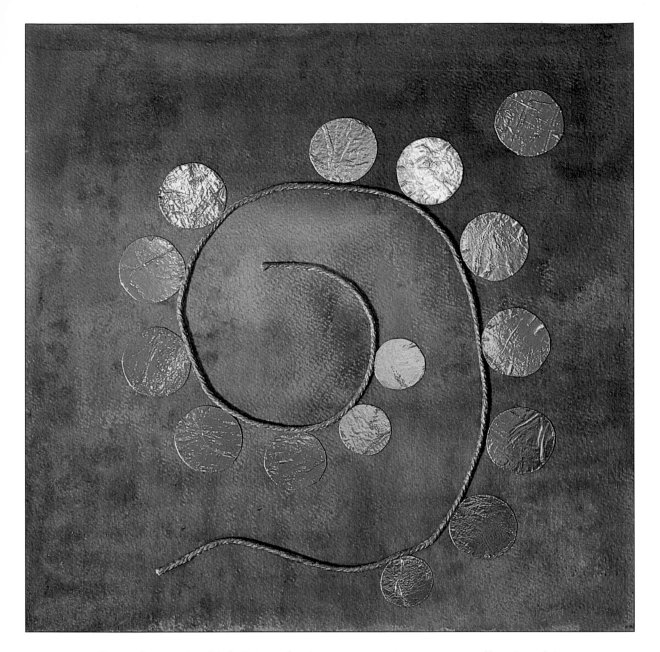

- You will need some gold foil (confectionery wrappers are excellent), white paper or card, a length of string and some glue. Paint the string with gold paint or a gold felt pen if you have one.
- First make the coloured background. You can tape the paper down before you paint it if you don't want it to crease as it dries out. Sponge-paint the paper with a bright colour to contrast with the gold coins.
- To make the coins first smooth out your gold foil and glue down onto a thin piece of card or plain paper. Draw the coin shapes on the back of this and then cut them out. Arrange the coins and string in a swirling shape on the coloured background and glue down! Don't forget to leave one coin missing!

The Good Samaritan

One day a teacher of the law said to Jesus, "It says in the law that you should love your neighbour as you love yourself. But who is my neighbour?"

Jesus told him this story to answer his question.

"One day a Jewish man was travelling down the lonely road from Jerusalem to Jericho. Suddenly robbers attacked him, stole his money and beat him up. They left him lying half dead at the roadside. After a while a priest came along but when he saw the man he crossed the road and walked on by.

"The poor man lay in the hot sun waiting for someone to help him. Soon a man who worked in the Temple came down the road. He looked at the man but then he too crossed the road and hurried on.

"Then a Samaritan came along on his donkey. Now Samaritans and Jews were not usually friendly but when this Samaritan saw the man, he stopped because he felt sorry for him. He got off the donkey and tore up some cloth to make bandages for the man's cuts and bruises. He helped the man on to his donkey and took him to an inn where he could stay the night. Next day the Samaritan said to the innkeeper, 'Here is some money for you to look after the traveller until he is well. If you need more, I will pay you next time I come this way.'"

Jesus said to the teacher of the law, "Which of those three men acted like a neighbour?"

"The one who was kind to him," said the teacher.

"Then you go and do the same," said Jesus.

- You will need some fabric for this picture – felt is used here, but any plain coloured fabric scraps will do. Donkeys don't have to be grey!
- First paint a rocky background scene using hot, dry colours. Crumple and glue down brown paper to create a rocky foreground. You can add bits of dried grass or kitchen herbs as here to add interest.
- Cut out the donkey shape from felt and glue down. Add string for the harness, and either snipped fabric, or wool, for the mane and tail. Give the donkey a brightly coloured blanket and your picture is finished!

The Farmer and the Seed

One day there were so many people crowding around Jesus that he had to sit in a boat at the edge of the lake while the crowd stood on the shore.

Jesus pointed to a farmer sowing seeds of wheat in his field. "Look at what happens to the seed the farmer sows," he said. "Some of it falls on the path at the edge of the field and the hungry birds swoop down and eat it up. The farmer walks on, and some of the seed falls on stony ground. It may start to grow but when the hot sun shines on the young plants they will wither up because there is not enough soil for the roots. The farmer moves on up the field and scatters more seed which falls in a patch of weeds. The weeds will grow faster than the wheat and they will choke it.

"But some of the seed sown by the farmer falls into good soft soil. The rain will water it and the sun will help it to grow. After a while the farmer will have a good crop of wheat."

Jesus explained later that he is like the farmer and what he teaches is like the seed. The ground is like the people who listen to him. Some people hardly listen at all to what he says, others listen but go away and soon forget. Still others start to live in God's way but give up after a while because it is too difficult. But some people listen to Jesus, understand how God wants us to live and go away and do it. They are like the good crop of wheat and God is pleased with them.

- In addition to paper and paints, you'll need some twigs, a handful of rice (brown or white) and some puffed rice cereal for the stones. Broken pasta or pieces of paper could be used as an alternative here.
- First paint the scene with hand, sky and soil. Try to make the good soil look darker than the rest. Glue down the stones and twigs. Paint thorns onto the twigs to make a patch of prickles.
- To create the effect of the seeds falling to the ground just dot glue over the area between hand and soil, and scatter the rice over the glue generously. Press down and wait a few minutes before shaking off excess rice.

Jesus often went to the Sea of Galilee. Sometimes he sat in a fishing boat by the edge of the sea and taught the crowds of people who came to see him. He often crossed the sea with his disciples. Some of them were fishermen. One night when Jesus was not with them they worked hard all night but caught no fish. Next morning as they came to the shore Jesus came along. You can find out what happened next if you look up John chapter 21 verses 3 to 6.

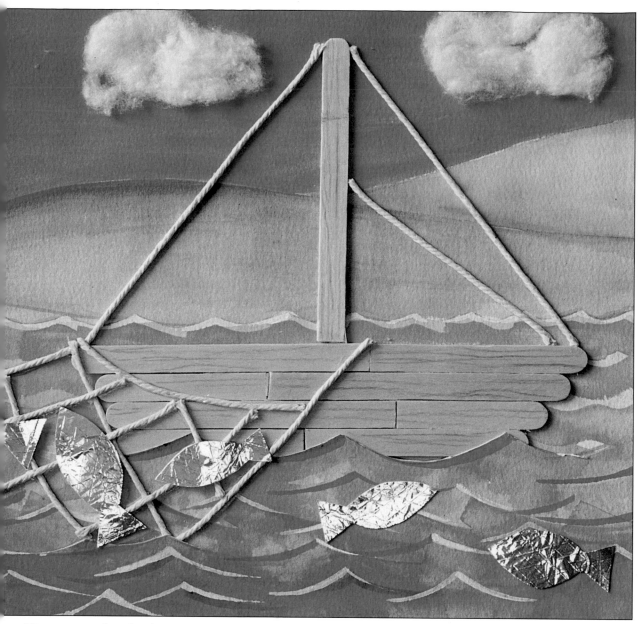

How to make the boat picture

Paint a scene with sea in the foreground and some hills and sky behind. You can paint wave shapes into the sea to make it more interesting. Make a simple boat shape from lollipop sticks (you can buy these from craft shops). If you want to trim the sticks you may need help from an adult with a strong pair of scissors. Stick the boat down one piece at a time, tucking the bottom pieces into the sea as in the picture above. Just cut along a line of waves to do this.

  Then make the net and the boat's ropes from pieces of string, and you are ready to catch your fish! Cut fish shapes from baking foil, sweet wrappers or shiny card. Glue them on to the net to give a 3-D effect. Add some cotton wool for clouds. Cut one or two simple boat shapes from card and stick them in the background to finish the picture.

The Buried Treasure

One day Jesus was teaching the people about the kingdom of heaven. Jesus wanted them to understand that it was not like an ordinary kingdom on earth. He told them that they could not see his kingdom because it is in people's hearts. Those who live as Jesus wants them to are making him their king.

So he told a story about a man who was out walking in a field. The man suddenly tripped over something which was sticking out of the ground and he fell over. He got up and went to look at what had made him fall. It looked like the handle of a pot. The man pulled at it but it was heavy and did not move. Then he scraped away the soil covering it and discovered that it was a large pottery jar. He tugged the jar free from the earth and looked inside. Imagine his surprise when he found it was full of gold and silver!

"This treasure is worth a fortune!" he exclaimed. "The owner of this field would be a rich man. I must see if I can buy the field."

The man carefully covered up the treasure again and went to see the owner of the field. The man agreed to sell it but the price was high.

"I'll have to sell everything I have to buy that field but it will be worth it in the end," the man thought.

The man was happy to sell all his possessions so that he could buy the field with its treasure.

Jesus said that joining the kingdom of heaven was like finding the treasure.

- Paint a background of soil and sky, then cut out the pot shape from a piece of card – cereal box card is good for this. Glue down the pot so that the plain side of the card is showing, and paint a terracotta colour. You can then lightly sponge over the pot with paler and darker shades to give a more 3-D effect.
- Make the coins by gluing down gold and silver foil onto card and cutting out into coin shapes (try using some different sizes!). Scatter these onto the soil around the pot, and add some pieces of grass for extra interest.

The Workers in the Vineyard

One day Peter, one of Jesus' disciples, asked him, "What reward shall we get for leaving our homes and our jobs for you?"

"Listen to this story," Jesus said. "Once there was a man who owned a vineyard. Early one morning when the grapes were ripe he went to the market place to look for men to come and pick them for him. He agreed to pay them a silver coin a day and they started work.

"Later in the morning he hired some more workers and agreed to pay them a fair wage. They started work immediately. Then he went out again at midday and at three o'clock and hired some more men. Towards the end of the day, at five o'clock, he hired some others in the market place.

"At the end of the day the owner of the vineyard told his foreman to pay the men their wages, starting with those who were hired last. They were paid a silver coin each. When the men who were hired first came to be paid, they expected to get more but they too were each given a silver coin. 'That's not fair,' they grumbled. 'We've worked a whole day in the hot sun and you've paid us the same as those men who have worked for only an hour at the end of the day.'

'I've paid you what I promised to pay you,' replied the owner. 'Are you jealous because I am a generous man?'"

Jesus was showing his disciples that God is kind and loving and always gives us far more than we deserve. We should follow him because we love him and not because we are looking for a reward.

- Paint a coloured background to contrast with the grapes. Glue down the background paper onto a stiff piece of card, as this picture needs more support than the others!
- Using the glue quite thickly, make a patch of glue in the centre of the paper where your bunch of grapes will fit. The glue should be transparent when dry so the shape doesn't need to be exact. Stick on pieces of shell pasta (conchigli) to create a really 3-D bunch of grapes. Leave to dry.
- When your grapes and glue are dry you can paint them purple (or green!) using a thick brush well loaded with paint. Take care when painting around the edges of the bunch.
- Stick on a stalk of green paper (you can paint this), and then add some tendrils by cutting long strips of paper which can be curled by winding each piece tightly around a pencil for a minute. Arrange artistically!

The Worried Disciples

Jesus knew that sometimes his disciples worried that they might not have enough money to buy food and clothes. After all, they did not have paid jobs. He wanted to tell them that they should trust God and not worry.

One sunny day as they were walking through the fields, Jesus said to them, "Just look at those lovely wild flowers. They don't work or make clothes for themselves. And yet their petals are even more beautiful than a king's clothes. If God dresses them so well, can't you trust him to provide you with clothes too?"

A flock of little birds swooped down and landed on a tree by the roadside.

"Do you see those birds?" Jesus asked. "They don't plough fields or sow seed. They don't have barns to store the harvest in but they sing happily and don't worry. God takes care of them. Don't you think that you are worth more to God than a little bird?

"So there is no need for you to worry about money or clothes or food. Your Father in heaven knows that you need them. If you live to please him, he will provide what you need. Some people set their heart on getting rich so that they can buy lots of clothes and have lots of money. But when moths eat the clothes and robbers steal the money, they have nothing left. If you set your heart on pleasing God, it will be like storing up treasure in heaven where there are no moths or thieves."

- In addition to your painted background you will need some spaghetti for branches, thick white card for the bird and flowers, and green fabric for the leaves.
- First paint the sky scene with a sun in one corner, then cut out your bird shape. Cut out varying lengths of card for the tail and wings. Make a slit in the body of the bird to tuck the wing feathers into, but first decide where your bird will be on the background. Glue it down and before the glue is dry, quickly slip in the tail and wing feathers as shown on the picture. Then you can snip the ends of the wings and flick up to give a really feathery effect.
- Stick down the spaghetti to make the branches, and then cut out simple flower shapes from the same white card. You can gently bend these with your fingers to make the flowers lift slightly from the background. Glue them down and add a few green leaves, and your picture is finished.

23

The Ten Girls at the Wedding

In the part of the world where Jesus lived, weddings were quite different from today. In the evening of the wedding day, the bridegroom and some of his friends would go to the bride's house. The bride and her bridesmaids would be waiting for them, dressed in their wedding clothes. They would form a joyful procession back through the streets to the bridegroom's house. Then everyone would join in a feast.

Jesus told a story about ten girls who wanted to join in a wedding procession. They had brought their oil lamps with them but only five of them had brought extra oil with them. It got quite late and there was no sign of the bridegroom. The girls were tired and fell asleep. Suddenly at midnight there was a shout: "Here he comes! Get ready for the procession!"

The girls scrambled to their feet and grabbed their lamps. The oil was almost finished in all the lamps but the wise girls put in the extra oil they had brought with them. "Give us some of your oil," the others said but the wise girls said, "No, we can't because there won't be enough for you and for us. Go and buy some for yourselves."

While the foolish girls went off to buy oil the procession set off to the bridegroom's house. The wise girls went inside, the door was closed and the wedding feast began.

At last the foolish girls arrived and knocked on the door. "Let us in!" they shouted. But the doorkeeper said, "Go away! I don't know you."

"One day I will come back to this world," Jesus said. "You don't know when it will be, so you must be ready."

- You will need play-dough, plasticine or children's modelling clay for the lamp, some tissue paper, and silver foil.
- First make the lamp by rolling out a thin piece of modelling clay. Glue it into place on your background paper and incise a pattern with a pencil or crayon. Paint a flame shape with glue and press the tissue into it to add texture – you can dilute the glue with water a little so that it soaks into the tissue and this should dry hard to give a firm surface to paint on.
- When everything is dry you can paint the flame and the background. Make some silver foil stars and a moon for the window to show that it is night.

The Lost Son

Jesus told a story about a father who had two sons. When he died they would inherit all his money. The younger one came to his father one day and asked him for his share of the money now. His father gave it to him and the son said, "Right! Now I'm off to enjoy myself!"

The son soon made friends who helped him to spend his money. But one day the money ran out and the friends disappeared.

"I'll have to find work or I'll starve," the son said. So he went to ask a farmer if he could work for him.

"You can look after the pigs," the farmer said. The boy was so hungry he even wanted to eat the pigs' food. As he sat watching the pigs the boy began to think of his father and home.

"Even the servants have enough to eat at home," he said to himself. "I've been very silly. I'll go back home and ask Father to forgive me and to take me on as a servant."

So he set off on the long walk back home. His father used to watch the road every day, hoping that his son would come back so he saw him while he was still in the distance. The father ran to meet him. He hugged him warmly but the boy said, "Father, I don't deserve to be your son."

His father took no notice. "Bring some clean clothes," he told the servants. "My son was lost but now he has been found. It's time for a party!"

"God is like that loving father," Jesus said. "He loves to forgive those who are sorry because they have done wrong."

- In addition to paper and paint you will need some rubber or upvc glue, and an old toothbrush and comb!
- To make the mud at the bottom of the picture just squeeze on thick strips of glue. This may take a while to dry but should give a raised effect. Then you can paint on the background – brown over the glue to create mud and a splashy loose yellow above.
- Cut out your pig from paper and paint it pink. Paint a thin strip of paper pink as well, for the pig's tail (you can curl this by winding it around a pencil). Draw a face and ears on your pig and glue on the curly tail.
- Mix up a nice muddy brown colour with paint in a saucer. Now take your toothbrush, dip it in the paint, and flick it across the comb. (Make sure you aim at the picture!) Repeat this process until you have a very muddy pig!

The Determined Friend

One day Jesus was teaching his disciples about praying. He told them this story to show that God is always ready to listen to us, but sometimes we have to wait a while for the answer to our prayer.

"Just imagine that a friend turns up at your house. He wants to stay overnight but you weren't expecting him. You have no bread in the house and he is hungry. Although it is midnight you decide to go and ask a friend to help you. You knock on his door and call out 'Friend, can you lend me three loaves? A friend has just come to my house and I've got no food for him.'

"And suppose your friend doesn't open the door but calls out, 'Go away and don't bother me! We're all in bed and the children are asleep. I'm not getting up at this time of night to give you anything.'

"What would you do? I think you would keep on knocking and shouting until he did get up and give you the bread. Even if he didn't do it because you are his friend he would do it because you kept on asking him.

"God always hears us when we pray. We may need to keep on praying about something but God is our loving father who knows what is best for us. If a son asked his father for a fish, would he give him a snake? Of course not.

"In the same way, when we pray to God, he will only give us things that are good for us."

- You will need some string, an old sponge and some oatmeal for this picture.
- First paint the background to contrast with the loaves. You can add interest by using two toning colours and brushing them on in different directions using a wide brush.
- Make the basket by cutting lengths of string and gluing them down firmly. You can weave other pieces of string through as here, to make it look like a real basket.
- Ask an adult to cut the sponge pieces for you. They will need to use fairly large scissors to cut slices from the sponge. Then the sponge pieces can be shaped carefully by trimming with scissors. Again, a grown-up should do this.
- Glue down the sponge pieces and paint over with a pale brown paint. When this is dry add a little glue and scatter some oatmeal over the bread.

The Great Feast

Jesus was invited to dinner one day by an important Jewish leader. There were a lot of other people there too and one of them said to Jesus, "Won't it be wonderful to be at a feast in God's kingdom!"

As a reply to the man, Jesus told this story.

"Once there was a man who invited a crowd of people to a great feast.

He made all the arrangements for the food and on the day of the feast he sent a servant to remind the guests that it was time to come.

'Oh,' said the first one, 'I've just bought a field and I must go and look at it. I'm sorry I can't come.'

'Sorry! Can't make it,' said another guest. 'I have bought some oxen and I have to go and try them out in the field. Please pass on my apologies.'

'Well, I've just got married,' said another one. 'I'm afraid I really can't come to the feast.'

And so it went on. All the people who had been invited to the feast made excuses.

When the servant went back and told his master all this, he was very angry.

'Right! Go out into the streets and invite all the poor people and all those who are disabled to come to my feast. Go into the country lanes and invite anyone you meet so that the house is full.'"

Jesus was saying that God is like the man who gave the feast. Everyone is given an invitation to join God's kingdom but not everyone accepts.

- You will need some play-dough or children's modelling clay, and some scraps of brightly coloured fabric, or felt.
- First paint a contrasting background and glue this down onto some stiff card. Then roll out your modelling clay quite thinly and cut out the bowl and cup shapes (a pastry knife can be used for this).
- Glue down the bowl and cup, and incise or paint a pattern on the bowl (the cup too, if you want!). Cut out some fruit shapes – grapes, pomegranates and apricots would have been eaten in Jesus' time. Glue these down.
- To finish, paint some red wine in the top of the cup. Then use either cling-film or clear adhesive tape cut to shape over the top of the wine to make it look liquid.

Here is where you can find all the stories in your Bible.